SLEEPER

HOLD

SLEEPER

JIBADE-KHALIL HUFFMAN **HOLD**

FENCE BOOKS

Cover photograph by Paul Salveson
Book design by Jess Puglisi

Published in the United States by Fence Books, Science Library 320 University at Albany, 1400 Washington Avenue, Albany, NY 12222

www.fenceportal.org

Fence Books are printed in Canada by The Prolific Group and distributed by Small Press Distribution and Consortium Book Sales and Distribution.

Library of Congress Cataloguing in Publication Data
Huffman, Jibade-Khalil [1981-]
Sleeper Hold/Jibade-Khalil Huffman

Library of Congress Control Number: 2014945618

ISBN 13: 978-1-93420086-5

First Edition.
10 9 8 7 6 5 4 3 2

Fence Books are published in partnership with the University at Albany and the New York State Writers Institute, and with help from the New York State Council on the Arts and the National Endowment for the Arts and the Fence Trust.

CONTENTS

NIAGARA

On the first day
of the poem

we perform
a trust exercise, on

the next day we all
start dancing in the street.

There is a moment of silence
during which

everyone traded clothes
you were just beginning

to come into your own
when you have to adopt the speech

of a telemarketer. When
we all come to

you say, "it's been so long
since I've had

a good laugh
at your expense

when was the last time
You told a joke

that wasn't a veiled reference
to your beliefs?"

On the third day of the poem
the graph showing our decline

is played by a tarantula.
The boy is played

by a method actress.
Our theme song

is the Star Spangled Banner.
On the surface of nature

is an argument
for crying your eyes out

and a coupon
for more disaster.

On the fourth day
of the poem

we retire into
a glacial haven, pleasantly

as an asthmatic
Gladys Knight impersonator, as

an Elk of the earth, a Shriner
of the earth, a husband

of a daughter
of the American Revolution.

I will spend
part of infinity

as a migraine
colored rush

barreling as always
into a room of children sleeping.

I am secretly in love
with a girl who tells me

"I haven't heard
a saxaphone breakdown

in a while
so I'm going to put on

this Carly Simon record
and see what happens"

I'm going to carry
the tune

of an imaginary latitude.
As the star of

an undercover operation.
At a time of

a scarcity of gloves."
Ominous territory

in which a middle aged
everyman coming unplugged

inside a wall of sound
inside your asshole

otherwise I imagine
the rest of the bad guys

hiding as they have
in the wild west

burying their name
for the internet

then appearing
as that person

in real life.
I haven't been attacked

for a long time or
for a similar beginning

or else I've
torn down the sign

and started over
with a different parachute.

I am in love
with a girl

who calls everyone
into a huddle

and gives a speech
to motivate them

into believing
they are rich

and tells everyone
to put their hand in

and say "Antartica"
on the count of one hundred.

At the count of five thousand
everyone ought to

pour buckets of Gatorade
onto the fire.

I'd like to
give myself enough hand jobs

until I can forget
I'm in love

with a girl
who says

"Before Gossip Girl
there was Edith Wharton"

Norman Mailer and
Vietnam started out

at the same time.
In a declension of assholes

in the middle of
a frenzied weekend

of mapping
the Bermuda triangle

in the time when
Jupiter disappeared

at the dawn of
the life of its many moons

every day
a new brand

of vodka
is invented

in America.
Nothing matriculates like surrealism

where I go into
a different octave

and say "it's all over.
Anyone can see

the planets are
inedible bodies of work"

and you tell me
that's the highest thing

I've ever said.
You don't know

if I'm really
there anymore

to tell you about
what happened

on the last show
in a special

twenty-part episode
of Judge Judy.

We only
talk about blasphemy

to distract ourselves
from the tension

in the air.
To a build a fortress

around our hearts
I don't know

why I do the things
I do.

I'm going to
go to sleep

and wake up
and watch "Daria"

for a while I'm sure
you know

where you have been
and can describe it for me

in several languages.
I know what you did

last night and the
night before Christmas

You can barely
have one, how can you

tolerate both or even
several of them

in a knife fight?
Much as I fantasize

about having hate sex
with captains of industry

same as I've taken
to fleeing to the edge of town

my life
is the opposite of yoga

the same as
jogging when

someone is chasing you

POEM FOR CEDRIC
THE ENTERTAINER

White people
love the 1980s.

Black people
can't help

but strive for
more declarative sentences

"my life
as a dog" "My life

in the bush of ghosts"
and other advertisements

for cunnilingus.
White people

have their drugs
on the front of their shirts.

White people
cannot stop talking

about Duke University
as if it is

the only place
that exists.

Black people carry their wives
over the threshold

then set them down
in a tub of posies

and go back
to the lobby for more.

Black women are especially sassy
in the poems of Howard Zinn.

White people
are always wearing

hats that say "disco fries"
"my other hat

isn't a hat at all
but a catamaran

manual in disguise."
"I'd rather be

inside you than
a parishioner in the church."

"My other hat
is a calling card

for musk
and Axe Body Spray

and sometimes the bill
for thunder and lightning."

MY SUPER SWEET SIXTEEN:
THE MOVIE

The Wings of the Dove

In their house at night it looks like a man is hanging from the chandelier. It's no wonder our daughter has the codeword to get in the nightclub; we never pay attention to anything when we spy on them and then we can't make up our minds about what to have for dinner. We don't know if our daughter was home or out passing bad checks. She'd already forged our names on the permission slip for the field trip to the zoo and on the petition for making our swimming pool into a national monument and in the contract making our house into a bed and breakfast. We've had our fair share of brushes with the law and nearly solving the mystery, the years after our neighbors noticed a difference in their living room between the chairs and where they'd left them. We are trying to get in her good favor in deciding who she'd live with. In the training exercise that is itself a simulation of playing tennis. Which is really a television program of people taking notes in case they divorce.

Surveillance

My wife spends the first hour of her day monitoring everyone's telephone calls and spends the next eight hours playing the horses with her inheritance at the track. I usually spend most of my time watching my wife and most of the evening trailing her in a rental car. I spend the last hour looking at my neighbor being photographed, thinking some accomplice, out of view, was taking the pictures until I see him release the shutter with his hand by a cord running down to the floor and taking his picture over again, until he puts his pants on and starts acting in a sex tape with his wife and a man I imagine that they met at the airport.

The Wings of the Dove

I am afraid of what I will do in my sleep. As the plane goes down, when everyone is leading their children to put on masks after they have done on their own, in the years that I persist in the manner of an expert on heraldry and the author of the survey, of the question on a scale of one to ten how much do you know about the flames guided to find you. We surrendered our weapons at the gate but what about the fire extinguisher under the jump seat of the flight attendant and what if I curl the in flight magazine and batter the man beside me and use karate to get in the cockpit and take control of the controls.

NOW THAT I CAN DANCE

Instead of watching
a woman repeatedly
dropping her glasses
on the floor of the subway

and two people
sitting near her
reaching to help
each time she drops her glasses

and each time
they bump heads
and say sorry
and laugh about it.

Instead of Major Dad
why not

just watch
these commercials.

Your love

was going to take us higher

into space
and get us

into "Spanish"
and get rowdy
after the fact

when it was silent
after the rest of

the vitamins were chewed.
Our mechanism

for removing

our drawers
is the only thing going
so far as
tomorrow is concerned
with bated breath
someone

has to know
where they think
they can rent a van
and cop a feel.

Your dream
is necessarily

someone else's
idea of good fun
and
moreover
useful
in several phrases
of the jaw

and some of
the time before
we get to the station
during which

much is revealed
about a troubadour
who'd been standing
in the background
the whole time
pulling the woman's glasses
with a string.

HOW I KNOW I'M HERE

The harlots are scrambling the balcony. I imagine I am burning incense and telling everyone what happened at work and I start by announcing I'd been fired. I always end up falling asleep with my clothes on, saying before I close my eyes, "I was framed for one hour for documenting the citizens being placed under arrest."

You have to get me out of your bedroom and hide my time here in the interim and branch out to find other ways of making money. No one has known "Diff'rent Strokes" like I've known, as I have quoted for the better part of the hour of the movie showing their feelings, for everyone and their children, the speech Nancy Reagan gave when she appeared on the episode where, it is forgotten, Dana Plato started manifesting the effort of an adult lifestyle when it is carried out by a teenager.

In my room there are soldiers I have grown. Tall men who rise from the bottom of rest to branch out to me. At their height they reach and feel the ceiling and crouch over, though there is room, though I have measured the top just right for them. Once they have it in their heads they are doomed to injury they begin to take precautions. Saying they ought to move their cars when they have walked me up this street and this street looks like your street, only here they ticket you while you are in the middle of driving.

Or they observe that practice where you are, but here they also tow you. Or they tow you, too, but here they take your car to a lot several miles away from town. Or you have to go out miles to the tow yard, but here the proprietor asks you to accompany him to a lecture at the university where the speaker that night, when asked what animal she would be if she were reincarnated, turned the tables on the man asking the question and the man said he would be a wolf and she said she would come back as a worm "so I could crawl up your ass."

EIGHT HOURS ARE NOT A DAY

The city was out of money. Everyone had run out of money so they sold space on the recording on the subway. When you came into the station the voice would say you'd arrived at Fourteenth Street and that there were two Churches Chickens on or near that stop or that there was a Foot Locker right there in the station.

Everyone was out of weed so they pooled their money and sent their friend to Vermont to see his guy.

I'd gone into a coma. I woke up a month later, having neglected my duties at the agency, where my office was now occupied by all the boxes for the files on Atlantis. I said to Henry, I said "What the fuck, Henry?" He was wearing the same shirt and tie he always wore but I told him he looked different.

"You were gone so Jarvis had us put the boxes for the Atlantis."

"So, what if I go home and how about then I give you the rest of the day to get this out of my office?"

"He wasn't expecting you back. He said you would've wanted it that way."

"Do you know what the first thing I said when I woke up? I said 'get me Jarvis.' Before I said anything else."

Henry started telling me what I'd missed while I was away, that the consensus was to involve the boss in a kind of mutiny, to oust him from power, to make him aware of what we were capable. I had come back at the perfect time, to join them and to use my contacts in the feds and with local law enforcement to arrange for this and so many other kinds of insubordination.

It was the future of erogenous zones, our waiting for the rain, our becoming disappointed and moving on to other activities.

It was the year they ran out of names for hurricanes, so they hired Jarvis—disgraced and by then some months into his being relocated to Florida—to make things up, so that now we have "Everyone," "Some of Them," "Prudence" and "You."

WE DON'T BELIEVE YOU,
YOU NEED MORE PEOPLE

When I was writing this talk
I would procrastinate
by fantasizing
about names for exhibitions:
Jibade-Khalil Huffman: "I Don't Think You're Ready
For This Jelly"

Jibade-Khalil Huffman:
"Hello, I'm Shelly Duvall"
Jibade-Khalil Huffman:
"Destiny Says:"

"You Could Stand and
Stare Out the Window"

Beauty says:
I've tried hiding your relief
among such vanities
as those
archived in harrowing wind.

My analyst says:
"we don't belive you
you need more people."

I want

what I already have
several times over

I've forgotten to

forgotten to already bleed.

I want to start this talk by talking about
how I came into a windfall that lasted
only thirty five minutes.

Because I am the author

of many of
the novelizations of Indiana Jones,
I want to start this talk
by talking about
waking up in Central Park and finding your clothes
on the person lying beside you.

Here is
the beginning of this talk. It goes something:

Something like:

"Water; skinning his knee."

This talk
is about
geometry
important tones, important

chapters of the tones—
each of these
characterizing
a fitness. Of his knees:

Betrayal
is a singular truth

delayed response

more than often
absence

of looking for

something better to do.

This was
originally commissioned
in the service of
finally turning a corner

and

delving in. To theater.

◊

Jessica Stockholder is an interesting case.

Michael Asher is an interesting case.

Acyrlic and latex
and
doors

space and

skin
to be emptied.

Day wandering along through the fields

mirror and all of. The materials.

That gold rope

that
five finger

ring rap

"Raft

of the Medusa."

What birds.

What birds
call feathers
are in our lives

other material.

Blind, crawling along

toward a vanishing point.
Until

it is decided

and is named

the same

and several months
dedicated

to its completion.

This:
or that rock

some of

these chores

are a pleasure cruise:
life in

an outer space.

Professional
wrestling is an interesting case
because it can provide a spectacle
we can at once ignore
then
come back to.

At once ignore
and devote
our complete attention

because it has names like "Savage"
and "The Snake" and yet remains
a pagan altar.

Sheena Easton is an interesting case
since I was talking about this talk
and my companion said
she was the soundtrack to her dream.

Once

we go on
nothing can turn us back.

Not even

even mentioning.

To say nothing

To say nothing
of debutante.

Debutante

Jackie
Joyner Kersee.

Your biography
has brought you higher

than you ever
thought you'd go

flitting to and beyond

fact:

to ominous fact:

to
lighthearted congestions.

The capital.

The capital
of my body

is my heart.
The coastal region

is my skin
whose docks contain

this many ships.

One must serve

an expiration
to begin

to lather.
What plants

call vines
are desires.

You'll need to forgive me
ever saying

I'd tie myself
into a ship

staged on land.

Staged on land
everyone

thinks they know
something that

can solve a crime.

Take tense

show it to
your future self.

Your future self
can't contain

anymore
than he has lips.

Take tense
to a bridge

say you won't
decide he is

paintings of

forest fires.

Forest fires.

Frosted oat.

Vernacular.

Charming boat

on a sea.

Telephoned.

You're no one

'til someone

comes along

and punches you.

◊

The blues is an interesting case.

Because.

Because when you are listening
it doesn't seem
the rest of history
is sad enough.

There was
another talk
within this talk
about race films

There was
another talk within this talk
about a model U.N.
Model
United Nations.

Diorama.
Of the subplot
of juice impersonated

by blood.

Dario
Argento.

Jewel of the Nile.

There is
a sense within his films:
William

Wyler.
American

Indian.

World's longest
Soul Train Line World
Class Wrecking Crew.

Guinness book.
Duration
is an interesting case

I had explored
in this talk

for years

I have survived
to remake
"The World Is Not Enough."

I'm

every woman
because I'm supposed to be.

Chaka Khan is an interesting case.

Rufus is an interesting case.

Sheena Easton once described
flying as a symptom

of some larger threshold

we might carry on to.

Christ pose.

Jesus sneaks.
Hyperbole pills.
Jesus sneaks
out of a bedroom
so it doesn't
spontaneously combust.

My sister goes
after my mother, my mother goes
after my father who was upset
anyone showed up in the first place.

I wanted to call this talk:

Daddy.

Daddy

panties.
pedantic

cracker

"Ghost Dad"

"The Daddy Stroke"

Ghost dad.

◊

Here is
a talk about race,
its goes:

"Nicole Simpson
can't rap." It says, "some of us
rely on
other material.

What you can't hide
you will foreground
in the sentence:

"It's really hard
not to glare at the moon
in complete agreement."

This is
a thousand years
of sexual history

complete works
of Dudley Moore

performed

in Pictionary.

Dagwood

Bumstead:
"the gods
must be crazy."

When I am
comfortably seated
I whip my hair
back and forth
to save the day.

"Perfect Strangers."
Perfect symmetry.

No pedo:
I whip
my hair
back and forth
So I don't have to

walk any longer
than I have to.

We are
alarmed of
three-part harmony

a sect

ambidextrous.

This is
a saying
when it is

least appropriate

there was a time

I really thought

you loved me.
Your cruel heart

will get you everywhere
except into Exeter or
the Skull and Bones.

Cast in

the role of

Jeff Bridges' nemesis.
This is

a gluttony
you can send

out of spite.

You can know

one night
as a stand in
for the rest of
your sex life
until you
really start

really start

freaking out

you can think in

a faster capsule
than what's gotten you

transplanted
in similar feelings

on the grounds of
a sister city

we've pitched a tent
I want

to end this talk
with a series of hearings

to the applause
and general reeling

from the motion

of the ship

when it was

tipped over.

When it was

tipped over

I was raised
in a pleather garment

all pins and eyeholes

and dirty vests
patterned with sunset.

In this talk
the symbols

are alarming
in the fashion

we become

we've become

immune.

The symbols
are decided

in a draft lottery system

should you ever
ever line

all the cherries
in a row

it is considered
good luck to donate
part of your winnings

it was once
customary

to hide your money
behind the shelf

if you wanted
to end up anywhere

once night harbored
its roster of thieves.

We know now
that the end of the universe

that the rule
you keep deceiving
that the rule

like the sociopath

I know you are

that the capacity

for his ribs.

In the likelihood
of emergency

you can expect
a halter top.
You can
believe in

a green jalopy.
You can
rank yourself
among the great defenders
in NBA history

try to
convince them

we will say yes

to Kennedy

say yes

to becoming

a more realistic miracle.

"The Family
That Prays Together"

slowly disguises itself
against its best interests
in a plan to

corner the market
on the pills

for the strength
where my eyes
could see.
I like

the proposition

I like
the material
laid bare.

I've taken
Diane Warren
as my guide:

"Because
You Loved Me"
is really
a poem about
being regretful

for sleep mislabeled
"Because
You Loved Me"
once you start reading
and realize
there's no guarantee

no one is there
to field your complaint after five

on weekends, after six

in the middle
of "Jeopardy, during
a full moon, in
flagrante delicto
in

the middle

of dinner

when you call.

TROUBLE EVERY DAY

To those with
cables banded together

with the picture
fitting the description

to those
without whom

we wouldn't be here

one of you

is wearing a little
black dress

one of you

is brandishing
a cumberbund

talking along
about the whole thing

to the man in front of you.
There is at once

a spell of waves
and then a drought
of similar minutes

and the same night

we go home

the night

you had a bad time
everybody had
a bad time

you'd like to
start over
as personal trainer

then you'd
like to
succumb to a cliff
you'd like to
think you had a good run
until

everyone knows
everybody had

the same time
to convince the court
they were innocent
of going on tour.

You walked
a good walk
beside a troop
of gamblers
set up

in the dead end
in an expanse

of sunset.
There were the years
1998–2007
when Johnson held
the championship belt.

You kept in touch
with one of the gamblers
one time
you called and
met the next day.

You're right and you think
nowhere else
is in France.

Let's go

onto the clapboard

and start

in a different arrangement.
I love

meat lovers pizza
like I hate
improvised theater.

It could
be yours
and
so you go
and get in
trouble every day

besides

it will
be a long time
before you realize
you are talking
to Robert Longo that

you aren't
wearing underwear
that you
are always the person who says

in a year you'll be married
and having an affair
with your secretary

when people say
if you told me
a year ago
I'd be married
and having an affair
with my secretary
I would have told you
you were crazy.

TEEN WOLF / TEEN WOLF TOO

If you play the end of "Casual Diamond" and you segue into Waka Flocka Flame's "Hard in da Paint" over the beginning of the movie "Waiting to Exhale," over that films already great soundtrack and you stop playing "Hard in da Paint" and give in and call me, the songs match up perfectly with the film. The silence, then the dial tone, the conduct of the call is the same as the scene in the film when Angela Bassett's character, Bernadine, after collecting her estranged husband's things, sets fire to these belongings now packed comfortably in the husband's BMW. The act of setting the fire is enough but it is the way that Bassett walks away that makes you forget about anything else that happens in the movie.

I like to masturbate to pictures of pregnant women. I write to television actors and people in movies and ask them for advice. I write to Oprah Winfrey and I ask her for a job. I ask Richard Roundtree to make me his personal assistant. I get a letter from one of Oprah's assistants saying that while Oprah appreciates my initiative she can do no better than offer me some of the products she has given away on the air. I live off the money I make at the restaurant and between the shift meal and selling a set of watches Oprah's assistant sends me I don't have to spend any money for the first six months we live in Florida.

I save what I make at the restaurant and I buy myself the complete first season of "Jake and the Fat Man" on DVD and stay up most of the night watching the first ten or so episodes and the next day I go to the store and I come back with ice cream and many kinds of chips. I take off my bra and put on slippers and sit at my desk and write a letter to the president of Party Metropolis, after I call, after I am, at various points, ignored and yelled at in the course of trying to get my money back for a product they insist I cannot return. Once they hang up on me and I call back and curse out the woman who'd hung up on me before.

In my letter to the president of the company, I write about my mother's commitment to making the best product that you can make. I write down some of her favorite sayings, I write down the one about animal cruelty and how it could be prevented by corporations issuing full refunds to consumers who wish to return a strobe light and disco ball combination. I write down another one of her favorite sayings and then I dedicate a whole paragraph to my favorite, to the one about calling again and calling again as a means of sustaining the conversation.

We are in my room, in the bedroom I converted into an office, when we hear CBS has exploded, over the radio, after I am the one-hundredth caller in the race for tickets to see Johnny Mathis. All of the other networks are running the footage over and over and running the commentary of a leading expert.

"This is the end of history as we know it. This had to happen, this could have been prevented with a more concerted effort from everyone in the community." Another commentator passes out on the air, so flustered by the catastrophe that he cannot continue speaking and barely manages to sign off before he goes under, when they still have five minutes before they are supposed to go to commercial.

I put on a pair of sweatpants over the cheerleading outfit I was wearing to make fun of you and your desires. I turn off the television, and you put on a recording of a jailbreak on the tape deck and we make out and fall asleep.

This is what I sound like on the radio first thing in the morning. This is what I think about when I think about fucking you. This is what it feels like when I'm jerking you off.

I tell you I am thinking about enrolling in courses. I say I want to start thinking about a degree. I go online and spend twenty minutes Googling myself before I lay down on the couch because of the heat.

I go online again later and see that you have been placing ads using my feet. There is an email in your inbox and when we go to dinner later I have to admit that I know your password and then I have to start over by apologizing before I ask you again about using my picture to save us a place at a party for swingers.

I have always wanted to cause a scene.

I take up my wine glass but then decide to drink it. I pick up your dinner as if to press it in your face, but then you get up and run out of the dining room and when I see you later you are walking along the road so I stop for you and take you with me.

I live off the money I make at the restaurant and between
the shift meal and the sorbet and refrigerator and the
set of watches I don't have to spend any money on food.
I buy myself the complete first season of "[_____]"
and nod off when my boyfriend invites me to sit in on
his class where he is explaining his dissertation to all the
other graduate students in his department. His professor
asks him to repeat himself when he finishes and he tells
the professor to forget everything he just said. He says,
"Okay, so imagine you are robbing a bank. Do you go in
with a gun or do you go in threatening that you have a
gun in the note you give to the teller and when she reads
that part of the note, when she looks up, you pat the front
of your coat as though you're hiding something." He says,
"Most people say they would go in with the note because
most people haven't ever fired a gun."

After his class we go to Caroline's for dinner. His professor
asks him to stay after and offers to take us out to celebrate
but I remind him we already have plans with Caroline.
He invites his professor, expecting him to not accept but
he says yes and we all go in his car. He plays a talk radio
station he says he always plays at a high volume. He tells
us the first thing he did when he got a cell phone was to

call in to one of the shows and voice his concerns about Bill Clinton's appointment for the vacancy on the Supreme Court. He pulls onto Caroline's street and changes out of his blazer into a sweater vest he has me pass to him from the back seat and before we go in he asks us to tell him how we like the town since we can vote in elections now that we have been here long enough.

Caroline tells the professor she saw his wife in front of her in the drive-thru teller line at the bank. She was having some words over the intercom with what at first was just the teller but quickly escalated into the manager pleading with her to return the plastic capsule where you put your deposit and they sent back your receipt, through the tube, and if she complied the manager would give her back her driver's license. The professor says,

"Do you know that my wife is a first degree black-belt."

"Do I know? Like have I heard that in the street?"

"Exactly."

We try to outdo each other. My boyfriend tells a story Caroline immediately tops with a story about her sister getting her hand slammed in a door. We go around the table and say the latest news we have heard from the capital. We talk about the private lives of the House of Representatives. One of us goes on like he knows them because he was a freshman when the man in charge of our district was a senior in college and they had a class together. I don't say anything for an hour. Whenever anyone asks me a question I put food in my mouth and by the time I finish they have moved on to another subject.

If you listen to the soundtrack of "The Wizard of Oz" while you look at publicity photographs of Pink Floyd and you watch YouTube videos of Pink Floyd playing live on mute while you listen to Judy Garland sing through the sheets covering the television and you start telling your story in third person. If you give you and your boyfriend the names Linus and Lucy in your story and you make Lucy a dashing heiress and Linus a detective "who only knew the tenets of the gun." Playing "The Wizard of Oz" while you listen to Pink Floyd's "Dark Side of the Moon" is of course the most famous incident of histories colliding in perfect sync. When it was discovered that if you listened to "Dark Side of the Moon" while you watched "The Wizard of Oz" and you were presumably bombed out of your mind, it was reported on the news. Linus and Lucy get in bed and when they wake in the morning Linus is gone. Linus usually got up around noon, walked around in his pajamas for a while, cleaned the bathtub, made some calls, called Lucy, took a shower, met Lucy for dinner, went home, fooled around on the table, went to bed. Lucy tried to be as quiet as she could, once she was up in the morning, during that time she was a substitute teacher by day, an aspiring playwright by night, an actress in the evening hours, a maker of breakfast occasionally, the participant in a car pool after a while, the culmination of several months of riding the bus when Linus was using the car. She would substitute for middle school English classes, she would tell you, if you asked her, that her favorite students were the honors students, one of them brought her a card on the last day, the regular teacher of the class having missed the last six weeks having major surgery, the card saying that he appreciated what she'd done, the card being or having on the other side a reproduction of [_____], the card coming attached with a phone number, which she should call, at her earliest convenience. Lucy tried all the rooms again. She told herself Linus was hiding, he was going to jump out at any time with a |_____| commemorating some anniversary she'd forgotten, their ninth anniversary of first getting burritos, their fifth time getting ice cream headaches, the second anniversary of waking up together and saying this was going to be the day we would really try starting to leave.

We see a man on the street with a series of signs relaying his situation to everyone who passes and another man stops and reads the signs like they are cue cards.

I tell my boyfriend. On another day I tell him we have to evacuate the building. When we get to the car he says he has to go back he forgot to turn off the oven and plug in the charger for the drill. We have lived in this apartment since we started living in Florida. We can only get the landlord on the phone on the days we owe him money. On the afternoon we moved in our neighbor introduced himself and his wife and told us his plan to quit his job at the plant and a take the test to join the police. His wife didn't say much but kept wringing her hands when we expressed anything remotely close to concern over our new surroundings. She pleaded with us to not go but then remembered she was in our apartment. My boyfriend tells them they are welcome to stay but the wife says it's time they went and picked up their daughter from Vacation Bible School. At the door the wife invites us to her church and my boyfriend immediately accepts, forgetting that I'd planned on setting the alarm to watch the finals of Wimbledon.

On Sunday morning I sometimes go to Denny's and get takeout and use a second TV tray beside the one on which I am eating for an assortment of beverages, Gatorade and Bloody Marys and carbonated water. I can't remember another time I wasn't home, sleeping off the night before and all of that day really, when I started drinking at noon. I tell him, after our neighbors have left, that I hope he remembers I haven't gotten up before all the religious programming has gone off the air, when they are airing secular shows. I fall asleep on the couch for a while, when I wake up they're showing "Xena" and I get up to change the channel. I haven't been to church since I moved away after high school and I tell him that I don't plan on starting now, so she goes to church without me, telling our neighbors I've come down with something and he has forbidden me to get out of bed.

In the middle of the service he goes out to the bathroom and gets in the car. He drives to the strip mall near the church. All of the stores except the video store are closed. The man at the counter says, "Can I help you find something?" When he comes in the clerk's on the phone and when he tells him, "no," he goes back to his phone call. He looks at the new releases, what he can rent once she is by our apartment. He reads the synopsis on the back of the box of all the volumes of "Faces of Death." He drives back to the church and goes in with the congregation in the sanctuary. The only thing he can think to say is that he ran into someone he knew on the way back from the bathroom. After the service is over he goes with them to a buffet in the strip mall near the video store.

When he finishes his soft serve he tells them he has to go. In his car he turns on the air conditioning. While he is in the car, before he drives away, he sees the husband come out and smoke a cigarette. When he notices my boyfriend in the car he goes over and motions for him to roll down the window.

"I'm really glad you came."

"Well, I'm glad I came."

He opens the door and gets in the car. He pulls out his cigarettes, offers him one, asks him "do you mind?" when he light up a cigarette. He says,

"Of course I don't mind. But I only smoke when I finish a chapter of my dissertation."

"That's what I'd call living in moderation."

"And at parties."

He remembered once again that he wanted to go home. He said, "I need to go home." He asked him where he went during the service.

"I ran into someone."

"By the bathroom?"

"We had a lot to catch up on."

"Where did you go during the service?" he says.

"To the video store." He says,

"I used to go to the video store. There used to be drug store there, I'd look at the magazines. Now I've just given up and stay the whole way through."

We are aged thirty-one and twenty-eight. We have had a number of discussions with people who have stopped us on the street about how much we look alike. When people see us in a more innocent embrace they assume we are siblings reunited here for the first time in years, in this park for their benefit, in brightening their day. Whenever we start kissing someone gasps, which, for a time, we found thrilling though now it's just become another thing to complain about. How we would go to bed all the time but haven't slept on the same side of the covers before today, the day my boyfriend comes home from church and follows me into the bedroom and starts taking off his clothes. He says, "So, now I'm going to start taking off my clothes," and I tell him I hear a siren coming and someone knocking and ringing the bell. I get up and put on my robe and answer the door. There's a man I've never seen asking if he can come into the apartment.

He says, "One of our guys got hurt." He's wearing a jumpsuit like the other maintenance men wear around the grounds of our apartment.

He tells me he needs to use the phone. I say, "Come in." He says, "thank you" and walks past me into the living room. I show him where the phone is, in its cradle on the wall in the kitchen. He dials a long distance number and when I keep staring at him he stares back and eventually I give him his privacy. I go into the bedroom where my boyfriend has the blankets up to his neck though I can see him working his hands between his legs.

"Whoa, easy. There's a guy in the other room using the telephone."

He opens his eyes and closes them; he says "that has nothing to do with getting up in the morning or anything to do with romance," which is what I wish my boyfriend said more often or right before I went down on him or he went down on me or one of us did something nice for the other, where I start by taking off my shirt but when I make a move to get under the covers the maintenance man starts pounding on the bedroom door.

Outside the siren has become more sirens. Someone is speaking over a megaphone. One of the officers is saying they have the place surrounded.

You can tell the lights are more impressive at night, when these things usually happen. My boyfriend doesn't understand how he's had the same friends for so many years. When he goes to conferences in their respective towns he always emails them, expressing his desire to have coffee and catch up on everything. I can tell the maintenance man is the kind of man who feels the same way. If I stopped and asked him neither one of us would say anything for a while. He would still close the door, then lock it behind him, now that he is done with the phone, now that my boyfriend has put on his clothes and sat up in bed and put on his glasses.

I have a series of dreams where I am ascending a flight of stairs. I go up the stairs and there is one feather then there are deeper and deeper piles of feathers with each story. At the top of the stairs there is a bundle of feathers nearly blocking the door. On the roof my boyfriend is grilling vegetables. I know anything can happen in dreams but here's where it's different in my dream the next time I go up the stairs there is a marble and then there are more and more marbles. On the roof my boyfriend is calling long distance to Spain. In my dream, the next time I go up the steps there are bees and there is eerie music with increasing intensity with each story.

At the top of the stairs the door is swarmed with bees. My boyfriend opens the door wearing a beekeeper's suit and hands me a beekeeper's suit to wear over my pajamas. We go outside to tend to our bees and talk to the plants and brush our teeth. I usually wake up clutching one or more pillows, remembering some part of my dream but mostly just worried already this early in the day about how long I will have to stay here. It's great because we can provoke each other either way, to do good, to give different things a chance, to—in my case—stay up even later than before, to try drawing pictures of the Hamburgler when we got drunk, to—in his case—eating more grains and vegetables and no more going out with anyone putting money on pool. But then it's bad because it's so cheap. For what I paid later, when I moved to New York, when I got a room down the hall from a bathroom I shared with two Columbia law students, in Florida I got an entire apartment for me and my boyfriend, an office we like to roll joints in, access to a sauna and swimming if ever we wanted to do more than stay in for the usual time then leave at a varying, though altogether similar point sometime in the morning and return somewhere along in the evening, or this was my boyfriend's schedule until he went missing.

It's funny because we were in Berlin at the same time and didn't realize it until we started dating. He was on a Fulbright and never got out beyond the library and the bar where he took fingers of gin. I was living on some money my grandmother passed on. I'd said, in a now widely circulated and often misquoted email, I would never go back to college if the Delta Sigma Sorority was still in business targeting impressionable girls and the occasional street smart first year, straight off the bus from knowing how to get around town into a comfortable spread of wilderness blotted with pedestrians, a grid would have been nice in certain instances of wilderness, when we strayed from the party, woke up the next day and had to walk back in the wrong direction to get to the point when we can walk in the right direction, a grid is obviously the same thing as wilderness, it's great it's just one side is more reliable.

I told myself I was going to count to ten and when I got to ten I would ask him to leave. When I've counted to one hundred seventy five and I am right about to say something, there is a knock at the door. He makes me answer the door, there's a girl my age, blonde around the face, already explaining what went wrong in the very opening stages of coming through the door and being handed the maintenance apparel, a jumpsuit that matched his own even in name, as "Tom," on the space over the pocket. There is a girl who is calling in reinforcements, who is calling in favors to everyone she knows and there is a way out if you watch "Teen Wolf" and then you watch "Teen Wolf Too" right after you struggle out of a bondage situation and someone plays Conway Twitty's "Blue Eyes Crying in the Rain" after a comfortable silence you will start to feel like someone wrote this down then enacted it to settle a bet. There were two maintenance men waiting for a car in our apartment. A man named Jarvis was bringing a car and the plan was to walk out the front door, slip out through the crowd gathered behind a line of patrolmen, walk out of the parking lot into the road and walk until Jarvis picked us up. They had a description of the vehicle but they didn't know who was driving the cargo van that ran into the back of a parked convertible, the scene belonging to both the current rain of money and the previous scene of counting the money, the man counting the money, the majority of which was tucked in a suitcase, the rest about to be handed to the other passenger in the car and the reason for the cargo van knowing when to be there and the men in the car not knowing a van was about to smash into them. They said they had the place surrounded and they did certainly have a place surrounded, the apartment of a man we were pretty sure was selling drugs to afford always staying home and waving occasionally, whenever we are home during the day facing the windows of the following apartment across from us: in back of the oak trees, the cops demanding they give out and come outside with your hands up.

If you play the beginning of The Ronnette's "I Saw Mommy Kissing Santa Claus" over the first three minutes of "La Bamba" and you go over to a boy you know and introduce yourself. If you say, excuse me and step back to find yourself in the middle of a party, with the lights out as you imagined you would have at your party, five or six surviving members of the class of 2000, enchanted with staying up until dawn, with a television on in the background playing "La Bamba," if there are fog machines like you would have at your party, if everyone is talking about Lorena Bobbitt and you want to introduce yourself but can find no way into the information, if this is your party, if you listen to the middle of "[_____]" while you walk out to your car and you are thinking about the last scene in "Dazed and Confused" the thoughts in your head will sound the same as the dialogue in "Dazed and Confused." If you play Nirvana's "Drain You" while you ride in the back of a car headed out of here and the navigator in the front seat doesn't tell you her name but the driver's name is Danny, and when you fall asleep they are listening to "Drain You" and it coincides with the events in your dream and when you wake up they are playing "[_____]" and it's just like what you first see: the window going blurred with rain, the signs for podiatry, if you start talking about the worst rainstorm you ever had to go through and Danny hands you one hundred thousand dollars that cannot be found on his person when the cops pull us over and he keeps the key to a safe deposit box with the instructions to getting your boyfriend out of jail and you get it, the instructions to getting away once you give him the hundred thousand dollars at a later day, when there are no cops around, if you choose instead to get a ride to Minneapolis with your friend Wanda and you decide to take a bus north from there and settle somewhere in between, if you start working at the you should listen to "[_____]" when you invest your money, when you go here for years before you realize you had the same name but then it was associated with your explaining he was missing.

If you wake up another day in some other life. If you sit still in front of a mirror and say: I think the same thing: that he is bigger than me.

His room, compared to mine, compared to most rooms in Manhattan, is larger, though I do not, as he does, have to share my space with anyone since I moved here last year.

Before we were together as long as we have been, when he still had a roommate and we had to turn up the volume so his roommate wouldn't hear.

Before that I lived in New Jersey.

In Jersey City, which was easy enough in terms of getting to work but terrible as far as friends were concerned.

My friends all lived way out in the boroughs, mostly in Brooklyn though a few of them were in Queens. At all times at least one of them was living in the Bronx and that person was seen even less than me.

I got a new job as a personal assistant. I saved up enough money to make the first and last months rent on a one bedroom in a fourth floor walkup in the Lower East Side.

I meet him at a party and he tells me he usually doesn't do this: go up to strangers and ask them why they haven't met before.

I ask him, "well then what is it that you usually do?"

He excuses himself, comes back five minutes later and says, "hi, my name is whatever you want my name to be" and I say "no, really what do you usually say?"

Here is what he says.

Here is a quote from my boyfriend, and I quote: "But do you know who takes their job way too seriously? Security guards at chain stores. You know, who follow you around and look at you suspiciously and then this same guy or a different guy, I can never tell, is there to stop you and check your receipt at the door."

I tell him I have no idea what he's talking about. He says, "but then the guy doesn't want to let you go, though he has to since there's really nothing else he can do at this point. And then it becomes one of those times you think that this is a person you will probably never see again. You could say anything and it wouldn't matter. You could do something like tell him you like to fantasize about what animals imagine when they are being photographed."

I ask my boyfriend what he's thinking. I say, "what do you know about anything besides the New York Giants?"

We've had this argument over and over again to the degree it really isn't even an argument anymore.

I've started working on my memoir again.

I've lived in this town for a month and already I've joined a group of people who gather to talk about how much they agree about what do to with the government.

My friend shows me how to sell my bike on eBay.

My boyfriend asks me if we've gotten to the point in our relationship where he can cum on my face and I slap him until he begs me to start slapping him all over again.

He says, "when animals are being photographed they think about all the pictures they've taken with other animals and how it is unfortunate they never get to see what they look like."

NOTES

". . . so I could crawl up your ass" in "How I Know I'm Here" is paraphrased from Kiki Smith. The title of "How I Know I'm Here" is also taken from Kiki Smith.

"Before Gossip Girl, there was Edith Wharton. . ." in "Niagara" is quoted from "Gossip Girl." "Niagara" contains, additionally, a "Status Update" from Suzanne Richardson's Facebook page.

The title and phrase "we don't believe you, you need more people" is borrowed from Jay-Z.

ALSO

Portions of this book originally appeared in *Everyday Genius, Line: A Journal, Night Papers, Tantalum* and *After Stanley Donen.*

Parts of "Niagara" also appeared in *The &Now Awards 2: The Best Innovative Writing* (&Now Books/Lake Forrest College).

"We Don't Believe You, You Need More People" was originally commissioned by Steffani Jemison and Jeanne Gerrity and performed by Jibade-Khalil Huffman, Abraham Burickson, and Jeremiah Cothren at Southern Exposure, San Francisco, October 28, 2011.

"Teen Wolf / Teen Wolf Too" was originally commissioned by Mt. Tremper Arts and performed by Julia Frey and Jibade-Khalil Huffman, August 6th, 2011 at Mt. Tremper Arts, Mt. Tremper, NY.

A much shorter, earlier version of a very small section of "Teenwolf/Teenwolf Too" also appeared in the limited edition, "James Brown is Dead (Future Plan and Program)" as "Now That I Can Dance."

THANK YOU

Mom, Lauren Atlas, Kristi Dalven, Steffani Jemison, Nicole Katz, Ada Limon, Marci MacGuffie, Lauren Mackler, Eliza Newman-Saul, Mariah Robertson, Christopher Stackhouse, Kate Wolf, and Rebecca Wolff.

For the time and space to make (most of) these poems and stories, I am, as ever, grateful to the Millay Colony for the Arts, Ucross Foundation, Anderson Center at Tower View, Foundation for Contemporary Arts, Jerome Foundation, and Lower Manhattan Cultural Council.

ALSO BY JIBADE-KHALIL HUFFMAN

19 Names for Our Band   FENCE BOOKS
James Brown is Dead and Other Poems FUTURE PLAN AND PROGRAM

FENCE
BOOKS